Contours for Ritual

Contours
for
Ritual

POEMS BY MARTHA McFERREN

Louisiana State University Press
Baton Rouge and London   1988

Designer: Laura Roubique Gleason
Typeface: Baskerville
Typesetter: The Composing Room of Michigan
Printer: Thomson-Shore, Inc.
Binder: John H. Dekker and Sons, Inc.

10 9 8 7 6 5 4 3 2 1

The author gratefully acknowledges the editors of the following
publications, in which some of these poems previously appeared: *Helicon
Nine, Kentucky Poetry Review, Louisiana Literature, Negative Capability, Open
Places, Plainsong, Shenandoah, South Carolina Review, Stone Country,* and
Xanadu. "The Barometric Witch" was first published in *Sing Heavenly
Muse!* "Only the Order of Events Has Been Changed" previously
appeared in *Wormwood Review* (1986), Vol. 26, No. 4, Issue 104.

Library of Congress Cataloging-in-Publication Data

McFerren, Martha.
 A contours for ritual.

 I. Title.
PS3563.C3635C6   1987   811'.54   87-12486
ISBN 0-8071-1421-9
ISBN 0-8071-1422-7 (pbk.)

The paper in this book meets the guidelines for performance and
durability of the Committee on Production Guidelines for Book
Longevity of the Council on Library Resources.

*Publication of this book has been supported by a grant from the National
Endowment for the Arts in Washington, D.C., a federal agency.*

Logic is only another weapon
to get you what you want.
                    —Bill Withrow

                              I want the man to know
                    the miracle of the obvious.
                                   —George Cleveland

Contents

Acknowledgments

My thanks to Yaddo, where part of this book was written.

Thanks also to the people who've helped me assemble these poems: Heather McHugh, Lisel Mueller, Steve Schwartz, Lee Meitzen Grue, Kay Mettelka, and Alice B. Jacobs. My regards to Howard Nemerov for his continued support, and my love always to Dennis, who climbed over a lot of prehistoric monuments with me and picked me up when I fell off them.

Ideas for these poems came from a peculiar combination of sources, including *The Creative Explosion*, by John E. Pfeiffer; *The Happening at Lourdes*, by Alan Neame; *Peter Freuchen's Book of the Eskimos*; and *Ley Lines in Question*, by Tom Williamson and Liz Bellamy. I have visited a number of sites mentioned in this book and still can't say if the rocks are doing anything besides standing there being themselves. Some might say that's more than enough.

Contours for Ritual

We Know Where

for George Macdonald

North, though lean,
is never sophisticated.
North means entering a cave
discovered by a child,
as it's children who see caves
the way they see the Lady,
and North is a child's account.

The boy who tells you, *I believe
in two gods: Jesus Christ
and the Lord of Thunder,*
and shows you gravestones
with two sides, just in case.
And other small children,
unexplained in furs,
who sing like the highest wind
and show you wolves.

North is birds without color
and fish fermenting
in crevices along fjords,
and the sudden, astounding
evidence of wood
with its angelic grain;
where the wild hunt
that was never human
goes snarling along bracken
and the walls of those caves,
always in frozen flight.

You must go North
to get beyond North,
where the weather stops cold
and there is never rain
as we think of rain.
There one god or another
wastes stars, minor moons
and animals in too much sky,
and the one important moon
is milk in a bottle.

All this is what
you go away to
when the story is finished.
The storyteller says to you,
They thought he was dead
but we know where he was.
Somebody took him North.

Field Day

We got lost twice, went back
to Loughrea for some bad
pub grub, and then got lost
again, as the Irish do not
mark their roads, this being
a plot against Americans
who've turned their island
into a theme park and
made them serve us breakfast.
Some Tinkers ignored us; then
finally a sign said TUROE
STONE, though not where at all
it was, and the rain got drearier
and then we found it. There was
nothing but a field and the
rain and the stone and us.
Not even a shelter for the
confounded thing, though maybe
the Irish want their stasis
casual, as if it were a
cow patty. Well, yes, there
was a Gaelic / English sign that
said DON'T FOOL WITH THIS OR
WE'LL GET YOU, but it wouldn't
stop any tourist who travels
with a chisel. That stone had
to be always wet, like every-
thing else in Galway, but it
still looked okay: the usual
omphalos in its granite snood.
An old woman from the farmhouse
made us sign her book, and I
told her, *We just can't leave
it standing in the rain with
the rest of us.* She liked my
gloves, and she said, *Ah, it
was here two thousand years
before us, and it'll be here
yet.* She took our photos, too.

Her Side of It

Dirt under his nails,
grass clotted and broken
on his rough black sweater
and his throwing me
against that grass,
his two hands sliding flat
under my shoulder blades,
his fingers opening earth
the way he would my labia.
Down that sudden cleft
I fall headlong
as if the edges of my hair
were hung with knucklebones;
and falling, I see upward
in the closing light
those several struck heads
wedged half-rotted
in the seams of the well,
their burst mouths
dismembering to scream
GO GOoooooooo
though it was truly
that one inhuman voice
casting me away.

I've always known
changes weren't kind,
despite that prettiness
about life joining life
and sheaves bound in ribbons
under small stars.
I knew deep enough down
there was a sacred filth
wrapped in raw pelts,
and ten thousand cold years
multiplied by seasons
and divided by moons
not at all like
thirteen inviolate girls.
But I didn't notice

the soil under his nails:
the black origin, the grain,
that same old bargain
with necessary rot.
And he dropped me
into that.

The Best Advice I Received as an Adolescent

Doyle Downey would not stay
home in the afternoon because
the kids were all grown
anyway, so she would just
jump in her wide Lincoln and
head someplace. Not that
there was anywhere to go in
Gladewater, but she was the
sort of woman who could be
happy at Woolworth's looking at
the bugle beads. Her husband
said, "Doyle, we'll have to
put a steering wheel in your
coffin, because you won't stay
put when you're embalmed, either."
But I am telling you this
for what Doyle Downey said to
me when we were in a tight
space at what used to be the
Piggly Wiggly. She yelled,
"Honey, if I can park in it,
I can back out of it!" And I
have found this to be the
gospel with jobs, with men . . .

Horseflesh

Strange it's too noble,
except for dogs.
We'll nibble a pig
and risk the little worms
or dissipate a cow.
Watch out, carnivores,
we're dealing with meat
on its own terms,

whatever they are.
Things get ambiguous
in this green slaughterhouse.
Elite mounts elite
and keeps on going
like release and thunder:
all protein manes
and meat against meat.

Meat / Bread / Pie

We have problems; you have
problems—and meat.
　　　　—A wistful Russian

Too much metaphysics, hot
bread and pie.
　　　　—Rev. David Macrae

1

Come over and eat meat,
writes each immigrant
to the slowpokes.
Meat three times a day.
To eat cabbage
is to be a cabbage.

If the meat is bad
that is okay
because it is still meat.

Eating meat is
joining the militia;
not appetite
but obligation.
If meat is not safe
there is no safety.
The same for dollars.

When you are full of meat
you want some dollars.
You think of them as cutlets.

2

Bread is biscuits, actually.
If there is no meat
you make do with biscuits.

If the biscuits are bad
that is okay
because they are
only making do.

Biscuits are tough bastards.
In some counties they
whack dough with hammers
to get a rise out of it.
They always say,
You can beat biscuits
but not Americans.

Some never understand
democracy is not easy.
Neither are biscuits.

3

This is not the pie
they had in mind.
But then, the motto
of America should be
This is not
what I had in mind.
No, not at all.

Here the meat comes flat
and is not pie.
Pie three times a day
along with meat.
You have a right to pie.

If the pie is bad
that is okay
because it is still sweet.

You eat pie fast.
When you are full of pie
you are full of energy
to get what you want.

You know what you want.

Approaching It

The Japanese
sit tribally,
elbows at scapulas,
clavicles by knees.

They sit on wood
and look at white,
sit on stone
and look at inland sea.

They sit on clay
and look at quiet,
nibbling sashimi,
sipping minimal tea.

They sit in bundles,
unmovingly polite,
smiling past earlobes
at selected tree,
munching umeboshi,
small with each bite.

All without speaking,
meticulous, agree.
United by appetite.
Not singular
in what they
know to see.

Only the Order of Events Has Been Changed

I don't make up these
stories. I don't have to.
Just three days ago a
battery thief had a shootout
with the cops under our house,
and I slept right through it
because our air conditioner
is way too loud. Shortly
thereafter, Lee telephoned
to say that Moonyeen
in Australia had finally
managed to ship Reggie
that kangaroo head he wanted
for his skull collection,
but since it's illegal to
mail kangaroo heads, it
arrived in a box labeled
MODEL, WITHOUT GLUE. Then
I left the house, and
the woman next door had
ejected her drunken husband
onto the sidewalk and was
flinging his clothes at him
piece by piece, including
individual socks, and he
was taking potshots at her
with a heavy-duty Sears
staple gun. I decided
there were a dozen things
I should be doing and that
I should do them immediately.
But when I got in the Datsun
the words on the rearview
mirror said THINGS IN THIS
MIRROR ARE CLOSER THAN
THEY APPEAR, and then I
really began to worry.

Still There

Why have you done this?
begs the old shaman
of the Boston missionary.
Why have you made me
know I'm evil?

Why have you done this?
shouts Johnny Appleseed,
stalking from his trees.
Why have you told me
I'm not the wilderness?

The Boston missionary
sadly continues traveling,
knowing it's still there:
what the old saints called,
The duplicity of the Garden.

I Can't Sleep

New Orleans rots air conditioners
like San Francisco kills brakes.
"We'll buy a new one tomorrow,"
says Dennis. "There's this cult
that makes window units,
and it's in their religion
they have to use copper coils."
He says, "I want to snuggle.
I can't sleep if we don't snuggle."
"But if we do," I tell him,
"we're going to sweat
like two hogs in Chicago."
"Let's do it anyway," he says.
"I didn't get married to stay dry."
Which reminds me of that pilgrim
in Lourdes who was disconcerted
by the Virgin Mary decanter
where you pop the Virgin's neck
and pour out your favorite vino.
"Well," said the dear lady,
"we're not on this earth
to major in aesthetics." Any girl
who loves her daddy in his
plaid Bermudas understands.
I think our first aesthetic
came from moving. In the beginning
some bearded old insomniac
woke up his son and told him,
"My boy, there is but one god
and you are not it."
Not only was the kid not it,
the rivers, cows and cornfields
weren't it either. If god's nowhere
you can pack and leave home
and take the livestock with you,
and already you're less enamored
with what you'll find.
You're addled with changes.
Eventually you get something
called the Western mind,

which developed window units,
and this, among all units, happens
to be deader than Leviticus.
Damn. I wonder if there's any
couscous in the fridge.

This Woman

for Peter Freuchen

Aviaq has married
the Danish trader
who brought tea and needles
to eight families
north of the Sound.
A husband and wife
should agree, she tells him.
You say the moon
is a large, useless rock,
and so it happens
this woman will forget
the moon is a white bear.
And she gets on with dinner,
which is more important.

Leaving in 1927

The long curve
from Mobile to New Orleans
was hotter than
an overbaked croissant
and you dodged its flakiness
in the brown Gulf.
That wasn't relief,
it was only water.

And at sundown
you're in a hammock
on the old front porch
playing a ukulele
to that same heat
sweating through the screen,
and on the G7 chord
of "Ain't She Sweet?"
you have this wild urge
to just take off,
to pack your roadster
and head for twilight time.

You're not fleeing heat
because it travels with you,
nor fleeing a hurricane
because there isn't one,
though the idea of hurricanes
just could be enough.

Whatever the reason,
an off chord warns you,
"Clear out, honeychild.
Pack your jewelry
and thesaurus
and your grandmother's
Morocco traveling bag,
completely silk-lined
and with silver fittings
from the time
ladies cleared out in style.

Yes, sweet thing,
pack yourself and scram."

And by glory
this time you do it.
You grab a selection
and off you drive
into the Southland,
into mosquitoes and moths,
your windows open
and your mind far ahead.

You're Marie Antoinette
fleeing to Varennes
with a scarf on your hair
and a picnic basket,
knowing your crowded coach
won't reach the border;
or dead Nefertiti
in the night at Luxor,
being snatched by professionals
who'll unravel you
for a batch of scarabs.

Well, it's a change.
Anything for a change.
You could face death:
a feud, a rotten bridge.
Maybe a Klansman in purple
with a spectacular hood
will dash from the pinescrub
waving a torch.

You're very frightened.
You feel so very good.

Too Familiar

Delaney up there screaming,
"I kiss the parrot
on its horny beak!"
Me rubbing my thumb
on Dennis's knuckles,
just like I always do
when the poetry is awful.
And for one raw second
I thought my husband's hand
was Daddy's—the hair rougher,
the cuticle more eroded.

Of course the change
is from his crisp effort
at raising salad greens
plus a sudden resolve
to build that gazebo by himself,
and, naturally, Dennis
is growing older.
But I really did believe
he might turn and whisper
Daddy's own words: "God knows
why you want all this
but I guess I can pay for it."

Something

Have you ever had the feeling
you're walking past
something that isn't there,
but it is not there
with such indelible impact
that you wonder why you
can't see it not being there?
And the something tells you,
Of course you can't see me.
This isn't your world.
And you answer, Let's not
start that again. I'm on
pretty solid ground lately,
and with a great sense
of organization. I have
outlived tons of vegetables
and a few roots and herbs,
and I've got cousins
everywhere in the foliage.
So it is, too, my world.
And the something sniggers,
What do you want to bet?

The Barometric Witch

for Nancy Harris

Trust the equinox in your body.
It's the weather that's god
and was always god,
from its first naïve implosion.

It starts with a central air
and a crazy throw of language
that maybe convinces you
orbits jig at a few young words.

But it was never witchcraft;
I've known this focus
and I promise, it's only family.

Listen, I don't make bargains.
I hoot at sistrums and rituals
and when I hear of Mother-Anything
I clear out at once.

Yet I change if the weather changes.
I'm after the rock's concern,
tearing its innards, shouting,
Listen to me. I'm involved in this.

I've lain with my face in dust
like the limestone Nefertiti,
been banked under clay
in the flower crown of Shub-ad;
have cured in the acidy bog
in my long blonde ponytail
and beaten solar disc,
waiting for fascinated scientists
to take my fingerprints.

I've emerged from a rowan
like some moony dryad on a break
and spun across fields
in my green aromatic shawl.
But it wasn't my idea.

It comes with the weather
our god, this blue weight of air,
and I have no say in it;
no grudge against Copernicus,
no pity for the antlered king.
I'm here for the ride.

In the fresh launch of summer
I spread my fingers
on the planet's shoulders.
I gouge it, merge with it,
go when it rocks with synthesis.
This is the family business.

And now the ice is thickening,
an indifferent mirror.
Does it even see me
buried once again; this white cortege
the snow, this clutch of
red berries at my breast?

The Horse in Commarque

Sit in darkness an hour
thinking about red meat,
then switch on your flashlight.
The horse is always there
unless it's not.

Some braille the wall for hours
and never find the almost-natural
flaw of nostril, the rough cheek
rising like a limestone blister.

Then it reappears
in a few sly seconds.
Is that indentation of muzzle
a Paleolithic grin?

Maybe it's the angle of light
or whether you've slept well.
Maybe the horse is
up to something.

With his flat lamp
the sculptor crawled inch by inch
hunting a contour for ritual.
And he and the perfect edge met
and a snap in the dark told him,
This is a beginning. Do something.
The horse surprised him
as much as anyone.

So it comes and goes and comes;
you never know if
the horse is feeling possible.

What else do you have to do?
Crawl down and look.

The Selkie

The man, after all,
had seemed normal
despite the scent of salt
in crotch and armpit
and a slight verdure
of earlobe. But then
he announces he's a seal
and their child
will be a seal
at least sometimes.
She'd wanted a change,
but no catch
quite like this one.

She'd been needing
the land's end,
that icy disorder
no islander plays with
after hours. The excuse
of somebody paddling
like he owned the place,
calling, *The water's fine*,
was enough to haul her
into the sea's net.
She wanted cold.

The shock of going down
the first time
in a rawness you're told
is never your friend,
never your great love.
And after you've plunged,
wanting to learn
how much colder you can go
and what happens
when you reach there.

Not swimming with seals
and the easy kelp
or even becoming them,

but starting a current:
deep sea itself
distilled in its nucleus
to thickened fluid.
Not azure or green
but white, finally,
and heavier than water
ought to be.

Her mother's anger:
So now you know.
Now are you satisfied?
Satisfied to zero.
Except for not catching
the bigger fish:
the cold curiosity
that sets you paddling
in the Skerries
down past the light.

The Saga Continues

I fell off Dun Aengus
in the Aran Islands,
spraining my ankle
and severely bruising
other carnal items.
The guide yelled JAYSUS
like an Irishman should.

After he calmed down,
my husband thought
it was sort of adorable.
Any woman, he told me,
can fall off the porch
(I've done that, too)
but it takes real style
to bust your butt
on a Neolithic ring fort.

Reinforced by Paddy's
and a cane, I kept limping
another rainy week
through Lough Gur
and the crannogs,
since we bourgeoisie
can't afford to dawdle.
Yes, history needs me.

But you'd think
in this clash of cultures
I could have seen
the edge of a small man,
or a woman wearing shells.
Even the brief tapping
of flint on flint
would have been nice.

This wasn't an equal trade.
Sometimes I wonder
if I fell too quickly.
Or, possibly, too slowly.

Irish Skin

I did expect pallor:
a few bleached hearts
with a widow's peak and chin.

But the fluorescence,
that kept me wary.
Too easy to blame drizzle

and recommend Ibiza or
vitamins. It's more likely
some aging fire, like a

banked Samhain, which proves
the elf mound was there
behind our eyes. Or maybe

it's the draw of living
in too much time, which
does not emigrate, till we,

also, start believing
the ancient bunco
that time itself is white.

Irish Roads

The Irish elk,
also red-haired
and uncooperative,
has left for
legend: it couldn't
fit these roads.
I don't fit, either,
and this car is
smaller than
any antlers.
There was nothing
on T59 (if that's
where I was) but
elkless narrowness,
though I admit
being lost
and being all gone
aren't any closer
than cousins.
Another tourist
told me, *It's
Gaelic Zen:
the assumption
you must know
where you are,
or else you
could not be here.*
The truth is,
they don't want us
on their roads
which are on
their country.
I can understand
the disorder
of an American
under every rock
when there are
oh so many rocks
to be under; but,
people, if you

do not like our
staring at your
history, I think
you should not
have had so
much of it.

June 22

We saw it in the channel
Midsummer Day, leaving Mull
for Iona, St. Columba's island,
where he landed after that
prayerbook fracas in Ireland.
For some good reason
the water was completely in
stripes:
        aquamarine and azure
plus a warp of turquoise, though
the turquoise did not count
for much.
        I'm told most men
will never see these colors.
They won't admit the names.
You can't see what you cannot say
and men will not say *turquoise,*
azure, and *aquamarine.*
        Even
Columba, a saint, and wanting
his own way like every saint,
might never have seen those
colors like I said them.
        So
what's unnatural, the water
or the words? Or is the miracle
having two sexes?
        I asked my
husband, "Do you see the stripes?
There, in the water." Of course
he saw them.
        "What colors are
they, honey?" "They're all blue."

December 22

Maybe nothing's there
if you don't believe it.
The transparent frost,
the dead madonna tree
with its single arm
crooked around the moon
become only natural again.
The farther you draw back
the more they separate,
the more likely
pure hyperborean chance
set their molecules
in that particular carol.
And you have to draw back,
it's so cold here.

Maybe that suspended moon
is only a lantern
like those in the trees
during the old calendar.
Maybe whatever is
simply is, no matter
what you think.
But you have to move
or this clear night
will finish you
as surely as chaos would.
When you cross the snow,
does it matter or not
if you look up to see
a factor dripping stars,
coming to lift you
nowhere you'll recognize?

Don't Call Me

A practical breed, the Scots,
though considerate
in their own brusque way.
In the border ballad
when that boy lay dying,
slain by treachery,
he seized his killer's hand
and said, *Tell my father*
I'm away to school in London.
But no lies for his girl.
It was, *Tell her I'm dead*
and the grass is growing green.
He knew his father
had no other sons,
so let the old man hope
for holidays and good reports.
But a pretty girl,
she'll corner another man
if she hasn't squandered
her few hot years
fretting for the vanished.
Yes, time will screw her
unless she knows the facts.

But you, you're wondering
where I was all weekend
and why the telephone
only rings and rings.
Can't you remember
my family's from Glasgow?
And don't you feel the soil
on your two eyelids
and a dour lowland weight
against your breast?
Let's not be drubbing what's obvious.
Stay put, laddie—
the grass is growing green.

The Fall

It's always the same
when you're primeval:
you find something to chew,
make a little trouble,
do some magic that keeps
your specific vegetation
recycling at wet intervals.
Half the time you're mired
in spatial boredom,
seeing all sides
of the quarry at once
with never a surprise,
but there's satisfaction
in being the people.
The people,
oxygen's focus.

Sometimes god interferes
behind your right eye
and tells you
what's to be done—
whatever god is,
whatever done is,
whatever you are.
But you do it,
and if blood ensues
it's not your fault.

So it continues:
bread, peritonitis, music.
And then one day
you're snuggling together
watching the rain collect
in a dog's ear,
when this arid stranger
from the new business
of sheep and goats
comes wandering.
He munches a locust,

then suggests,
O my coagulated children,
have you ever
thought of going
in di vid u al . . .

Not Speaking Japanese

This language
is a samurai
who by concentration
takes virility
to such a focus
he is spared
all worry of women.

You learn the noise
to surpass it.
Never speak,
but ascend instead
to the eyebrow;
the tapping fan;
a certain incumbent
angle of the head.

Update for That Biographer

Martha McFerren, still hoping
for a biographer, abandoned
caftans and heavy earrings
and started tweed and glasses.
She wrote two books of poetry
but the major response
came from her husband,
who suddenly recollected
her year's leave of absence
had become three years.
He said, "I've done enough
for literature." She got a job.
At a party, designated subject
yelled, "If I see one more line
of stones-and-bones poetry
I'll absolutely croak,"
and four months later
entered her megalithic phase.
Also, she became prominent
throughout the South by saying,
"There are two things I hate,
nature and sensitive men,"
in front of several sensitive men.
She liked throwing GOD around,
and when she wrote MAGIC
she meant something else entirely.
Horses appeared on her page
with disquieting frequency,
as did ghosts and the Japanese,
and she wondered if she might
start seizing folk
by whatever lapels they owned
and telling them of
her childhood and her dreams.
She was publicly labeled
INSENSITIVE TO ESKIMOS
and thought it a likely epitaph,
but finally she hit on
WASHED BY MISTAKE, though that
would probably change, too.

The Merry Maidens

1

They enter the ring of stones,
cameras clicking: some students;
mums over from Brighton on that

well-named jaunt, the mystery tour;
a balance of Americans. All here
for slabs of prehistory,

ignorant of those letters
filed at the Bureau of Antiquities:
I assure you, gentlemen, I shall

be months re-establishing myself!
Oh, maybe a loose psychic is here
and eager, but he's disqualified

for bias. We're concerned with you,
singular caught tourist. You
who read superbly, whose intellect

is linear—not cochleate—and geared
for sequence. What's it like
when the earth within the circle

starts fidgeting and throws you
one wild party? What happens
if the spirals come after you?

2

Nineteen wicked flirts, says
the guidebook, got themselves
petrified for dancing Sundays.

They keep on dancing, which shows
their opinion of this god business.
In quartz petticoats they flounce,

playing toss with polarity,
vaulting any hedge in your brain.
And the music—that high uncoiling

in the middle ear! Is it the Maidens?
Or this wild rock the planet
making a geocentric nausea?

You're becoming standard nebula,
nougat-thick with stars; a thread
of DNA helixed like stairs

into a choirloft; a protozoan;
or the emphatic pulse of Bernadette
in her ring of Pyrenean shrines

scrabbling a lost, wet charge
she never believed would cure
a single blessed thing.

3

Will you write your angry letter?
Should you go for a long Glenlivit
to fix your stomach, or try a prayer?

A prayer to what, exactly?
While you're at the pub, deciding
that one, you might even think

the spirals, in their witless crash
opened this very planet and threw time
on its countless quick entrances.

And you—guest of *dans maen,*
the perpetual stone dance—can you
find a more reasonable music?

dans maen: pron. *dawn's men* (stone dance)

Circles

We can argue
with what's there
if we have to
and tell the
stone circles,
You have no right
to exist.
Why did people
bother with you
when they should have
worked at writing
and irrigation
and the long trot
into flight?
But I think
they had to get
the universe
in order first.
How could they
work in such a
cluttered room?
No, they had to
straighten out
flooding and
bleeding and
the cycles of
suspicious elk,
and the direction
you walk to
change a season.
They had to bring
moon and sun
under control
and learn to be
violent in
hierarchies.
So they set priorities
and got to the
small stuff later.
But deciding this,

I wonder,
If they had
the brains to
set it straight,
why were they
so damned brutal?
And I think again
and I shut up.

Sure Thing Bonsai

We seven will admire
this tree together,
knowing the seven of us
admire this tree.
We will study it
in jammed quiescence,
taking our photographs,
seeing the one refinement
selected for us to see.

And the tree is discreet
in its achievement,
worth the compromise
of green, pliancy and brown.
It's decided by tribes:
you may be singular
or the tree may be singular.
We vote for the tree.
Sit down.

November 1

It's getting darker
and the boy's still there
on his black, crunchy island
where they lit the leaves.
Everything's over now.
He ought to go inside,
but he's walking the burn
and walking the burn,
too young even to wonder
what started this bleak progress.

In a few decades
he can have the facts.
Meanwhile he's getting closer
to hard evidence:
a chill that spawns,
the moon coagulating,
a neighbor's Dalmation
howling like a wolf with ideas.

Come In

Take what you want.
It's stony December
with nothing much to see,
and the old imperative
Take it and pay for it
worms through the drizzle
like a brown, soaked tune.
On Skye the finest music
is in the barrows.
You know how pipers learn it.
They stand in the doorways
and they listen.

Go Away

This mess was hopeless
even before the Vikings—
with that new danger, money,
stuck to their armpits
with Danish beeswax—
sat down under the towers
and waited for starving monks
to throw down reliquaries.

And long past hopeless
when Henry's tough mother
Empress Matilda told him plain,
Don't bother that green island,
though eventually he disobeyed.

Cromwell, up to his crotch
in corpses, and shackling the rest
for cane fields in Barbados,
was heard saying, *This has been
a wondrous great mercy.*

A mercy, perhaps, for the grass,
which has been trying
to ship us out for centuries.
The rain has, too. In those years
when the palest of potatoes
withered to soft black stool
and two Fenians were hung
from each of the carved crosses,
couldn't souls in bodies
recognize eviction:
that fine, lilting panic
to abandon sod?

Maybe the small dark people
who sat crouching, eating
their fathers' hearts
with loony reverence,
maybe they were all right
since they barely weighted earth

with their slight stalking
and listening for breath.

But that freckled bunch
with the red ideas
and blaring hair on edge
were wider and heavier.
They crowded the open air.
And it hated the saints
who traveled, never seeing
the landscape for the souls.
The landscape was mad as hell.

Some places own themselves,
and we should be satisfied
to let them lie there.
Haven't you felt it?
The green wants us to leave.

Yet Another Tomb

Somewhere near Drogheda, 1985

Again, the bent back,
the long cool hunker
like a goose born backwards.
I damn those tribes
who would not be sacred
at major intersections
and damn myself,
always the tourist
bruised in something.

And I'm claustrophobic, too.
I could never worm it,
though I don't have to;
there's a lot of big graves
in the world.

They want us back.
And they get us, don't they,
with what's inside?
It's like circulation.
A stone series of dreams,
the jags and spirals:

abstracts of rain
fire and seabird
and the grass consensus
which never needed me,
not even when the granite
was first vivisected.

We used to call it
our summer house
and winter house,
the heaviest of quiets.
Through years and more
this jampacked silence
was what we had,

and all of it
was equally the middle:

the middle of nowhere.
That's why they were frightened.
Why I still am.

Advice for Eskimos

Beware anthropologists,
those neutral missionaries;
also skip sugar, small arms
and circumpolar prayer.

But these are minor items.
What's tea and bullets
after that first surprise,
the big warm visit?

Later you'll get back
to ivory, and vindicate
those frozen eggs
you munch like apples.

Please accept the value
of steel and nylon
and our rare silence
in this cold you own.

A Gauge for Stonehenge

One man's magic is another
man's engineering.
    —Robert A. Heinlein

North itself migrates;
stars waver and lose vocation.
What we measure rises and falls

with twitches in a galaxy
and only mathematics lasts,
plus a surge in our brains

moist with accumulated data.
There's a secret water around us.
It tingles through unworked soil,

through ganglia of bluestone
straining for the moon,
and we stand between these two

like pests between lovers.
Such ingenious pests we are,
scheduling this granite dynamo

on a thousand soft years
of chalk and fog, aligning water
and a floppy lunar orbit.

If the current's fantastic,
still we've corralled it
with serene, exact bullheadedness.

Put off writing. Forget plows.
This is much more important.
Here, concentrically, we set

our gauge of poetry, where language
radiates like toadstools;
determine by easiest geometry

the scale for love and its
unreasonable genetics. This is
stone excitement. On our island

we crave salt and structure,
we dowse the current
to show it who's in control.

Ask, What laid the current?
Make a guess. But we want to know.
How does migration know?

Tell Me

Meet a stranger by night
and he'll ask a riddle.
Why should he want to know
what's deeper than the sea?
Why does that troll ask
what's whiter than milk
when he could munch you
under the bridge
without philosophizing?
Stretch the metaphor,
says the bearded devil,
or else, pretty lady,
you're not god's—
you're one of mine.
But he, too, is metaphor.

To save yourself
keep them jabbering till dawn.
Match their riddles
to the infinite power
until they freeze in sunlight
or drop to befuddled ash.
Vocabulary's the answer.
Rise on specifics, pretty lady,
since language is god's earth
and god the better word.

Tell me: will you rise
till there's no metaphor,
no question, no god at all,
only a full definition?
Will you rise till there's
no false knight on the road,
only yourself
grown sharper than a thorn?